W9-BJS-633

WITHDRAWN

ELEPHANTS

Jen Green

Grolier
an imprint of

■SCHOLASTIC

www.scholastic.com/librarypublishing

Published 2009 by Grolier
An imprint of Scholastic Library Publishing
Old Sherman Turnpike, Danbury,
Connecticut 06816

For The Brown Reference Group plc
Project Editor: Jolyon Goddard
Picture Researcher: Clare Newman
Designers: Dave Allen, Jeni Child, Lynne Ross,
    Sarah Williams
Managing Editors: Bridget Giles, Tim Harris

Volume ISBN-13: 978-0-7172-6292-2
Volume ISBN-10: 0-7172-6292-8

**Library of Congress
Cataloging-in-Publication Data**

Nature's children. Set 4.
    p. cm.
    Includes bibliographical references and
index.
    ISBN 13: 978-0-7172-8083-4
    ISBN 10: 0-7172-8083-7 ((set 4) : alk. paper)
    1. Animals--Encyclopedias, Juvenile. I.
Grolier (Firm)
    QL49.N385 2009
    590.3--dc22
                            2007046315

Printed and bound in China

PICTURE CREDITS

Front Cover: **Shutterstock**: Victor Soares.

Back Cover: **Shutterstock**: Kitch Bain,
Chris Fourie, Jonathan Heger.

Nature PL: Peter Blackwell 17, Richard
Du Toit 10, Laurent Geslin 45, Tony Heald
46, T. J. Rich 9, Francois Savigny 34;
Photolibrary.com: Martyn Colbeck 6,
Don Enger 38; **Shutterstock**: Mark Atkins
29, Francois Etienne Du Plessis 18, Chris
Fourie 22, Duncan Gilbert 13, Robert
Hardholt 2–3, 5, 30, Michael Sheehan 14,
26–27, Snowleopard 37, Victor Soares 4, 21,
Steffen Foerster Photography 33, 41, 42.

Contents

FACT FILE: Elephants

Class	Mammals (Mammalia)
Order	Animals with a trunk (Proboscidea)
Family	Elephant family (Elephantidae)
Genera	*Loxodonta* and *Elephas*
Species	Savanna elephant (*Loxodonta africana*), forest elephant (*L. cyclotis*), and Asian elephant (*Elephas maximus*)
World distribution	Africa and Asia
Habitat	From tropical grasslands to forests, marshes, mountains, and dry places
Distinctive physical characteristics	Massive body, with a long, flexible trunk and large ears; male Asian elephants and both male and female African elephants have tusks
Habits	Elephants spend much of their time gathering plant food; females and young live in herds; young males live in small groups, while adult bulls are mostly solitary
Diet	Grass, leaves, bark, and fruit

Introduction

The elephant is the world's biggest land animal. Everything about an elephant is big, including its huge, rounded body, massive legs, enormous flappy ears, long trunk, and curving **tusks**.

However, there's a lot more to elephants than just their spectacular size and shape. Elephants are smart animals, famous for their long memory. Loyal and affectionate, they live in family groups. Elephants help many other animals, too. In the dry season, they dig deep holes that fill with water. These "elephant wells" provide life-giving water for many other animals to drink or bathe in.

An African elephant's sturdy legs support its great weight.

Forest elephants gather in a bai—a large clearing in the forest.

Three of a Kind

There are three types, or **species**, of elephants. The **savanna** elephant is the world's largest land animal. Its relative, the Asian elephant, is smaller. Scientists now recognize a third type of elephant, the forest elephant. It lives in Africa, like the savanna elephant, and looks like a mini version of its larger, African relative.

It is easy to tell the difference between an African and Asian elephant. The African elephant has very large ears and a flat forehead. Its back is slightly U-shaped, dipping down between the shoulders and the backside. Asian elephants have much smaller ears, a humped back, and a high domed head. They also hold their head higher than their African relatives.

Stomping Grounds

Elephants are only found in tropical parts of the world. There, the weather is hot all year round. Instead of the usual four seasons, many places where elephants live have just two main seasons—a dry season and a rainy season.

Savanna elephants live in many parts of Africa south of the Sahara Desert. They mostly live in tropical grasslands, called savanna, but they are also found in woodlands, dry areas, and high on mountains. African forest elephants live in the dense jungles of western central Africa.

Asian elephants live in India, Sri Lanka, and eastward into Southeast Asia. Asian elephants still live in the wild, but many of these elephants have also been tamed. These trained elephants help with all sorts of work, such as carrying people and shifting logs.

A baby Asian elephant demands some of its mother's food.

An elephant's brain—the biggest of any land mammal—weighs up to 12 pounds (5.4 kg).

Record Size

If elephants played basketball, savanna elephants would be top scorers. Standing up to 13 feet (4 m) tall, they would actually look down on the basketball hoop. And with their nimble trunk, they would have no difficulty slam-dunking the ball! Asian elephants would have more trouble. At about 10 feet (3 m) high, they are just the right height to knock their head on the hoop!

The world's largest land animal is also the heaviest. A big male savanna elephant can weigh more than 7 tons (7 tonnes). That's as heavy as six family cars! The females are usually smaller and weigh less. Asian elephants weigh up to 5 tons (5 tonnes). Elephants continue to grow throughout their long life. An experienced animal of 50 years or more weighs considerably more than a 20 year old.

Tale of a Trunk

An elephant's single most unique feature is
its trunk. The trunk is actually a very long nose
and upper lip. The trunk is equipped with at
least 40,000 muscles, making it extremely strong
and flexible.

At the tip of its long, slender trunk, the Asian
elephant has a single fleshy "finger." African
elephants have two of these "fingers." These
highly sensitive tips are used to pick up and
handle objects as small as a single blade of grass.

Like a nose, the trunk is used for breathing
and smelling. With its sensitive trunk, an elephant
can pick up the scent of ripe fruit a long way
away. Such a smell could bring a hungry elephant
running! Elephants that live in dry areas rely
on their trunk to find fresh greenery or to pick
up the welcome smell of water.

A savanna elephant's trunk might grow to 6 feet (1.8 m) long.

An elephant's trunk can hold about 2 gallons (7.5 l) of water.

A Hundred Uses

An elephant's amazing trunk has a countless number of different uses. It can push, pull, pick up, hold, and throw things! The trunk also comes in handy when the animal needs to give itself a good scratch.

An elephant uses its trunk to gather grass, leaves, and other food. It is used to help lift heavy weights, such as logs, out of the way. The trunk can also squirt water or dust when an elephant takes a bath. A baby elephant keeps in touch with its mother by hanging onto her tail with its little trunk. It takes at least six months for the baby to learn how to use its trunk properly.

Contrary to what many people think, an elephant does not drink water with its trunk. It does suck up water with its trunk. However, it then squirts the water into its mouth and swallows.

Magnificent Tusks

An elephant's curving tusks are actually long front teeth that grow well beyond its mouth. The tusks keep growing throughout the elephant's life. Both male and female African elephants have long tusks. Each tusk can weigh as much as 132 pounds (60 kg). Asian elephants have smaller tusks and usually only the males have them. Big male elephants are sometimes called "tuskers" for their gleaming tusks.

Like the elephant's trunk, the tusks have many uses. The animal uses these huge teeth to strip bark from trees and dig for roots in the ground. Both bark and roots are a favorite meal for elephants. An elephant might also gouge holes in dry riverbeds to find water buried below the surface. The elephant's tusks are made of a substance called ivory. People used to carve ivory to make tools and ornaments. In the past, elephants were hunted for their tusks, but now hunting elephants for ivory is against the law.

An elephant digs for minerals, which are an essential part of its diet.

An elephant walks
at about 5 miles
(8 km) per hour.

Mighty Feet

The elephant's stout, pillarlike legs support its great weight. An X-ray of an elephant's foot would show that this huge beast is always on tiptoe—a bit like a ballet dancer! The toes rest on a spongy pad, which acts like a huge cushion. Despite their large feet, elephants aren't noisy or clumsy. The design of the foot allows them to move gracefully and make little noise when they walk.

Elephants often have to cover large distances each day as they search for food and water. At normal walking pace they usually move slightly faster than a human walks. But if an elephant needs to, it can run at up to 25 miles (40 km) per hour by lengthening and quickening its stride. Elephants usually run away from danger when they are startled, but they have also been known to charge their enemies. A group of elephants all running together at the same time is called a **stampede**.

Keeping Cool

On the sunbaked plains of Africa, savanna elephants have a lot of trouble keeping cool. Fortunately, these elephants have two built-in fans—their large ears—which they flap gently back and forth to make a breeze.

A savanna elephant's ears are enormous and twice the size of those of its relative, the Asian elephant. The ears act like twin radiators, giving off heat. Just beneath the skin, the ears are crisscrossed with tiny blood vessels. As the blood flows through the ears, it releases heat through the skin of the ears. The blood in the ears is also cooled by the flapping. The cooled blood from the ears then travels around the elephant's body, which in turn cools the elephant's insides. Asian and forest elephants don't need such large ears because they live in shady forests.

A savanna elephant's ears might grow as long as 4 feet (1.2 m) from top to bottom.

Bath time is
also playtime
for elephants.

Fun in the Mud

An elephant's skin is very thick in some places. On the animal's back, the skin is more than 1 inch (2.5 cm) thick. In fact, scientists call the elephant—and other thick-skinned animals such as the rhino—a pachyderm (PA-KEY-DURM), which is Greek for "thick-skinned."

An elephant's skin looks tough and leathery, but in fact it is very sensitive. It can easily crack in the fierce sun. The sun is not the only threat to an elephant's sensitive skin. Elephants are also plagued by pesky flies, ticks, and leeches. So how do they care for their skin? By coating it in dust and mud!

Elephants like nothing better than to roll around, or wallow, in a muddy water hole until they are covered in mud from trunk to tail. The animal often finishes off its mud bath by blowing dust all over its body with its trunk. Splashing, rolling, and sliding in the mud are great fun, but they also have a useful purpose. A thick coating of mud and dust acts as a sunscreen and might also prevent pesky bugs from biting.

Time for a Dip

An elephant never passes up the chance to take a cooling dip in a river or lake. While bathing, it also drinks a lot of water. An elephant needs to drink about 45 gallons (170 l) of water every day.

In dry places, such as the Namib Desert in southern Africa, savanna elephants know exactly where to find hidden springs and pools that provide life-giving water. They cross huge stretches of barren desert just to get a drink.

Elephants are surprisingly strong swimmers. When crossing wide rivers and lakes, they often swim underwater, with just their trunk and the tips of their ears above water. The animal's trunk acts like a **snorkel**, allowing it to breathe even when its body is underwater.

Big Appetite

Elephants are **herbivores**—they eat plants. Their favorite food is grass, but they also eat fruit, bark, leaves, and even young trees. Asian elephants also eat roots and flowers. Most plant food is not very nourishing. An elephant has to eat a huge amount to fuel its giant body.

Elephants eat about 350 pounds (160 kg) of food every day. That's about 900 plates of salad! The elephant then needs a bathful of water to wash it all down!

Elephants spend up to 16 hours a day eating. That means by the time an elephant is 60 years old, it will have spent 40 years of its life just eating! Elephants feed mostly at dawn, in the afternoon, and at night. In between these times, they often snack as well.

Savanna elephants and warthogs mingle peacefully at a water hole.

27

Tough Eating

Elephants eat tough and stringy food. These **mammals** need strong teeth to mash up grass, leaves, and bark. Elephants have broad, ridged teeth called **molars**. They only have four working teeth at any time, but during their life, they will go through six sets of teeth! As the working teeth get worn down, new teeth appear behind them and move forward to replace the worn-out teeth.

The elephant's digestive system includes 115 feet (35 m) of tubing, called intestines, to process its food. As the food passes through the intestines, the nourishment is absorbed. The waste then passes out of the body—in jumbo-sized piles of dung!

Food takes 22 to 46 hours to pass through an elephant. Even then, 60 percent of the animal's dung is plant matter that hasn't been broken down, or digested.

The leader of a herd—
the matriarch—usually
retires when she is
between 50 and 60 years
old. She is replaced by
the next-oldest female.

Herd Life

Female elephants spend their whole life within a group of elephants, called a **herd**. Most herds contain about 20 elephants, but in good feeding spots several herds might join up to make one big group. Herd members take good care of one another. If one animal is sick, the others try to nurse it back to health. They might support its weight with their own body or stroke it with their trunk.

The elephant herd is led by a senior female. She is called the **matriarch** (MAY-TREE-ARK). This very experienced elephant decides when it is time for the herd to move on to a new feeding spot. And when the leader gives the signal to move on to another site, all the others follow obediently.

At about 15 or 16 years old, young males have become too old to stay in the herd. At first, they usually hang out with other young males in small groups called "bachelor groups." As they get older, they spend more and more time alone. Adult males are usually **solitary**—they live alone, except during the **mating season**.

One at a Time

The elephants in a herd follow their leader all the time. The matriarch leads her troop to food and water, along paths that have been worn by generations of elephants. As the animals move along the trail, they often form a long line. Each elephant places its feet in the footsteps of the one in front. Over time, they wear a path—just wide enough for an elephant.

Baby elephants keep to the center of the group. They walk between their mother's legs, which must be like keeping pace with a forest of moving tree trunks! When they get a little older they hold onto their mother's tail with their trunk.

A herd of elephants might walk about 7 miles (10 km) each day in search of food and water.

Trumpeting is just one
of several ways in which
elephants communicate.

Noisy Elephants

Elephants make all sorts of noises to "talk" to other herd members. Probably the best-known sound is trumpeting. Elephants make this deafening noise by lifting their head and blowing through their trunk. They trumpet when they are angry, excited, or surprised or when they get separated from the rest of the herd.

Elephants make a low, purring sound when they are content. The happy elephant holds its trunk straight down to make this low, rumbling noise in its throat. Zoologists—scientists who study animals—have discovered that forest elephants purr a lot to keep in touch with herd members that are out of sight among the trees.

Elephants also produce very low rumbling sounds that are too deep for humans to hear. These sounds travel a long way. Elephants use them to communicate over long distances.

Body Language

Elephants have many ways of communicating with one another besides making noises. One important way is through touch. Human friends greet one another by hugging, kissing, or shaking hands. A pair of elephants greet by sniffing each other and by draping their trunks over each other's back.

Elephants also use body language to express their moods and intentions. The position of the head, ears, and tail can all show how an elephant is feeling. A curious elephant cocks its ears and lifts its trunk. If it smells something exciting, its ears flap back and forth. If danger threatens, an experienced elephant warns the others by rapping on the ground with its trunk. The matriarch of a herd lifts her front leg to signal to the others that it is time to go.

Two elephants greet each other with their sensitive trunks.

37

Once a bull has fought off rivals, he can become affectionate with a cow—if she is willing.

Mating Season

Elephants can breed at any time of the year. Adult males, called **bulls**, join the herd when they sense a female is ready to **mate**. If more than one bull arrives, the two might fight for the chance to mate.

The bull and female, or **cow**, get to know each other by lacing trunks and making deep rumbling noises. Once they are well acquainted, they mate.

Human families have to wait nine months before a baby is born. For elephants, the wait is even longer—22 months. Experienced females in the herd help the mother-to-be when she is ready to give birth. They gather around the mother and encourage her as she gives birth. They then cluster around the baby, or **calf**, and gently nudge it to its feet.

Big Babies

Baby elephants are quite hefty. A newborn elephant calf weighs about 220 pounds (100 kg). It stands 3 feet (1 m) tall as soon as it gets to its feet. Adult elephants have hardly any hair—except for the long hairs on their tail, which make the tail look like a fly swatter. Youngsters are hairier. Baby Asian elephants have a clump of hair on their head that looks like a crew cut.

Newborn elephants are shaky on their feet. The older animals gather around to make sure no harm comes to the baby. At first, the baby is too weak to keep up with the herd. The group stays with the mother and her baby until the youngster is able to walk with the rest of the herd.

A calf can walk within an hour of its birth, although it is shaky on its feet for a few days.

41

A baby elephant plays with its food before eating it.

First Foods

The first food of all young mammals is its mother's milk. As soon as an elephant calf wobbles to its feet, its first instinct is to seek its mother's milk. The baby **nurses** with its mouth, not with its trunk. That would be like drinking through the nose with a straw!

Baby elephants drink about 20 pints (10 l) of milk a day. After a few months, the calf might try to eat grass, but it finds gathering the green blades with its trunk tricky. It continues to drink its mother's milk until it is at least two years old, and sometimes until it is as old as four years. Baby elephants grow quickly. By the age of six years, the young animal is about ten times as heavy as its birth weight.

Playtime

Baby elephants have a lot to learn about the world, their own body, and life in the herd. They learn by exploring and also by watching the adults. Curiosity can get a young elephant in big trouble. Luckily the mother and other females are always nearby, keeping a watchful eye. Elephant mothers are kind and affectionate. The mother encourages her youngster to try new experiences. However, if the baby gets out of line and throws a tantrum, she gives it a warning tap with her trunk.

Baby elephants love to play with other young elephants. At one year old, the youngsters tumble in the mud, spraying water with their trunks. They also play-fight, head-butting and charging at one another. That all helps the young elephant to learn its place in the herd.

Two young
elephants play
their favorite
game—climbing
over each other.

45

A charging elephant
will trample to death
any animal in its path.

Keeping Safe

Adult elephants are so large that they have very few natural enemies. Sometimes, a group, or pride, of lions will bring down and kill a solitary adult elephant. The youngsters, however, have several enemies. Asian babies are at risk of being attacked by tigers. Lions, hyenas, cheetahs, and leopards will all attack young African elephants.

If danger threatens, the adult elephants form a tight circle with the calves in the center. The adults lift their trunks and trumpet loudly. They also raise their huge ears like wings, so they look as fierce as possible. Faced with a herd of angry elephants, most **predators** turn around and run. If the enemy fails to take the hint, the herd might lower their heads and charge.

Growing Up

At the age of about ten years, an elephant is considered an adult. At that time, the young males leave the herd. Young cows are allowed to stay with their mother, aunts, and cousins. It won't be long before these cows are ready to breed.

Elephants are among the longest-living mammals. They can live for up to 70 years in the wild. During their long lifetime, most elephants breed many times. Once a female starts to breed, she might have a baby every two to four years. Some mothers, therefore, have a young calf as well as a half-grown youngster with them.

The future of wild elephants is uncertain. Although there is a ban on selling their ivory, many elephants are still killed by illegal hunters, or poachers, for their tusks. In addition, many elephants are losing their habitat as humans take over their land for farming. However, elephants roam freely in many national parks and reserves. These protected areas should ensure the survival of these amazing animals for thousands of years to come.

Words to Know

Bulls   Male elephants.

Calf   A young elephant.

Cow   A female elephant.

Herbivores   Animals that eat mainly plants.

Herd   A group of plant-eating animals,
                 such as elephants, horses, or cattle.

Mammals   Animals that have hair and nourish
                 their young on milk.

Mate   To come together to produce young;
                 either of a breeding pair of animals.

Mating season The time of year when animals come
                 together to produce young.

Matriarch   The experienced female elephant
                 in charge of a herd.

Molars	The large, blunt teeth that are used for chewing and grinding food.
Nurses	Drinks its mother's milk.
Predators	Animals that prey on or hunt other animals for food.
Savanna	A tropical grassland with few trees.
Snorkel	A breathing tube used by divers.
Solitary	Living alone.
Species	The scientific word for animals of the same kind that can breed together.
Stampede	When a group of frightened animals runs together.
Tusks	The two long, curving teeth that grow out beyond an elephant's mouth. Tusks are made of ivory.

Find Out More

Books

DK Publishing. *Elephant*. New York: DK Publishing, 2000.

Morgan, J. *Elephant Rescue: Changing the Future for Endangered Wildlife*. Firefly Animal Rescue. Buffalo, New York: Firefly Books, 2004.

Web sites

Asian (or Indian) Elephant
www.enchantedlearning.com/subjects/mammals/elephant/Asiancoloring.shtml
Information about the Asian elephant and a printout.

Creature Feature: African Elephants
www.nationalgeographic.com/kids/creature_feature/0103/elephants.html
Fun facts, a video, an audio clip, and more.

Index

52